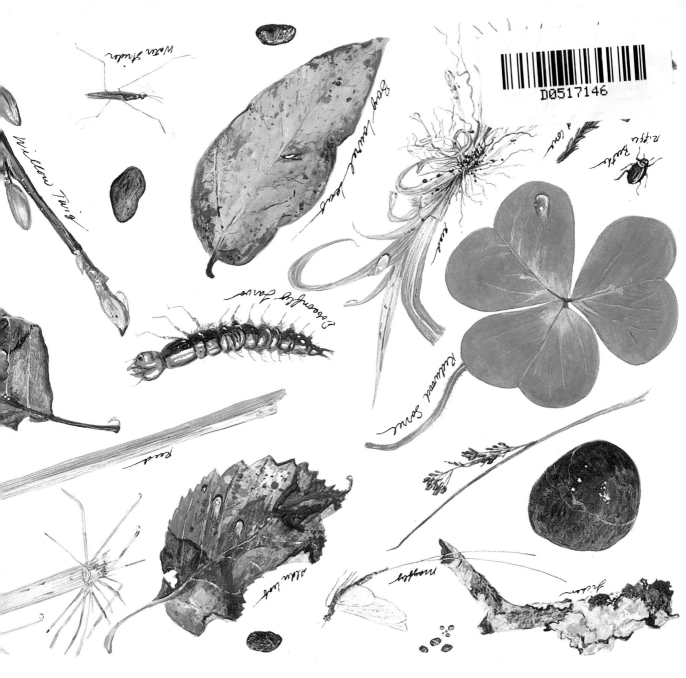

Learn More about the National Parks at the Golden Gate

Guide to the Parks
Ariel Rubissow Okamoto

Gardens of Alcatraz
Essays by John Hart, Russell Beatty, and Michael Boland
Photographs by Roy Eisenhardt

Published by Golden Gate National Parks Association
Available from the association or through your local bookstore.

WEB OF WATER

LIFE IN REDWOOD CREEK

Maya Khosla
Illustrated by Maryjo Koch

GOLDEN GATE NATIONAL PARKS ASSOCIATION
SAN FRANCISCO. CALIFORNIA

For Amy, who inspired this work

Library of Congress Catalog Card Number 96-78728
ISBN 1-883869-27-7

Editor: Amanda Hughen, Susan Tasaki
Designer: Jamison Spittler
Production Assistant: Diana S. Larrimore

Printed on recycled paper in Hong Kong through Global Interprint, Inc.

Contents

Preface

Some of my favorite stretches of Redwood Creek flow through Muir Woods National Monument. There, the air is a green curtain of leaves wrapped in light. Further upstream, cascades unleash their white and restless waters.

To salmon, Redwood Creek is a unique blend of features and smells whose mystery draws them in from the ocean, century after century. They have adapted to a specific combination of seasonal flows, temperatures, and odors unique to this creek.

Throughout the creek monitoring project in which I participated, I was continually inspired by the idea of being in the midst of these natural processes, many of which had been absolutely invisible to me before. Tiny winter wrens flitted from bank to scrub, uttering their high-pitched chirp chirp sounds; I watched them burrow their nests into the creek banks, in secret root-framed spots. Cobwebs twisted the light into glints of cotton-candy rainbows draped across the branches. The flow spoke of its mixed geographies and of the effects of season and life on its form.

Conducting habitat studies alone on the creek late into the evening, I rediscovered quiet reaches of cobble and boulder. One morning I found my backpack, lost days earlier in the creekside vegetation; along the creek's right bank, in the fern overhang and shadows, it sat on a tree stump. It was invisible until I was forced to slow my search to a crawl. Being alert to the creek quickly became habit with me.

A sense of discovery comes from spending hours in and around water. Can Redwood Creek change you, your existence? It changed mine.

REDWOOD CREEK WATERSHED

The watershed (in green on the illustration), land drained by Redwood Creek and its tributaries, is recognized as a special ecological area by the National Park Service.

MT. TAMALP

STATE PA

SHORELINE HIGHWAY

STINSON BEACH

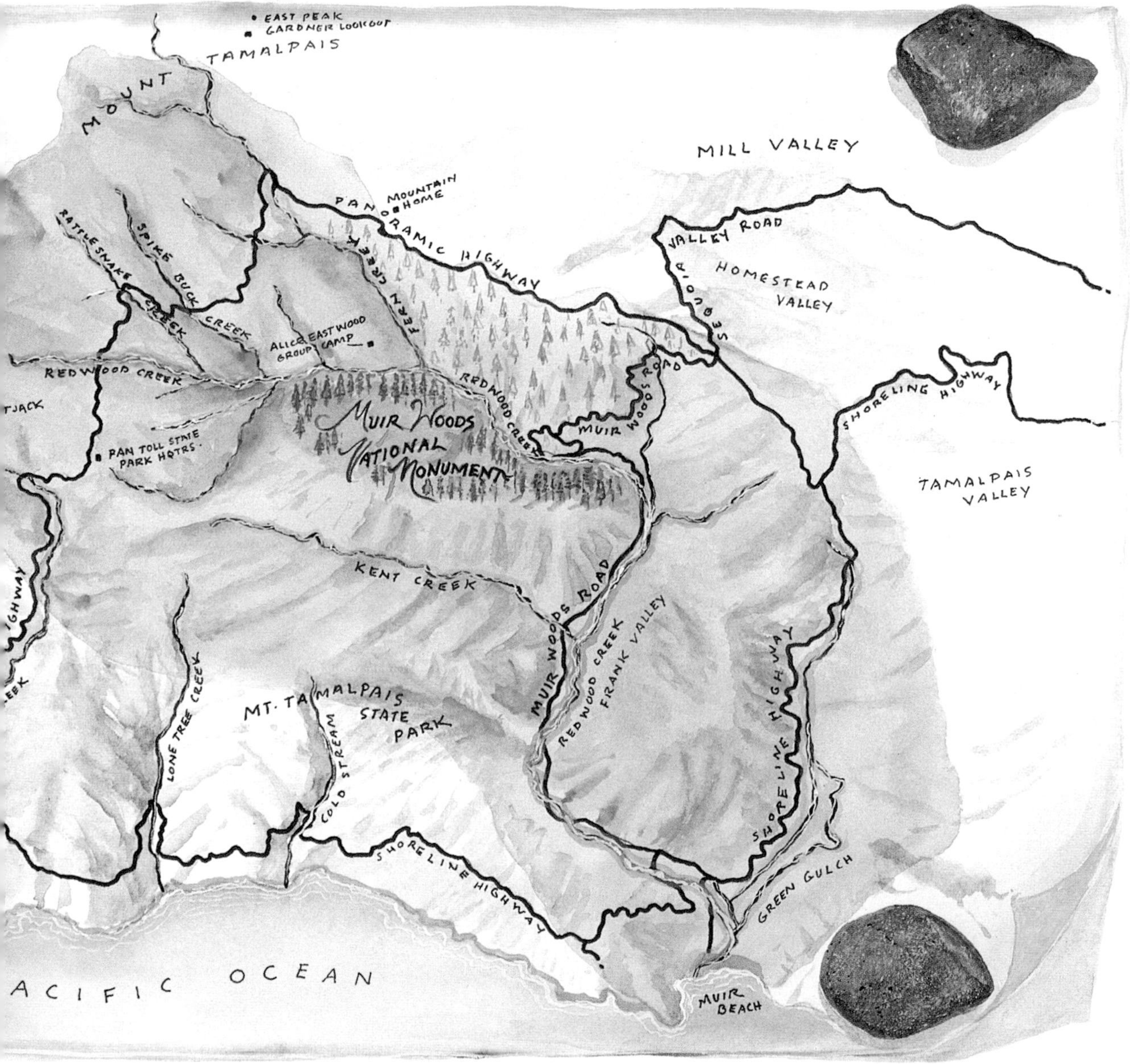

EAST PEAK
GARDNER LOOKOUT

TAMALPAIS

MOUNT

MILL VALLEY

RATTLESNAKE CREEK

SPIKE BUCK CREEK

PANORAMIC HIGHWAY

MOUNTAIN HOME

FERN CREEK

VALLEY ROAD

HOMESTEAD VALLEY

RIONIDO

REDWOOD CREEK

ALICE EASTWOOD GROUP CAMP

REDWOOD CREEK

MUIR WOODS ROAD

SHORELINE HIGHWAY

JACK

MUIR WOODS NATIONAL MONUMENT

PAN TOLL STATE PARK HQTRS.

TAMALPAIS VALLEY

HIGHWAY

KENT CREEK

MUIR WOODS ROAD

CREEK

LONE TREE CREEK

MT. TAMALPAIS STATE PARK

COLD STREAM

REDWOOD CREEK

FRANK VALLEY

SHORELINE HIGHWAY

SHORELINE HIGHWAY

GREEN GULCH

PACIFIC OCEAN

MUIR BEACH

Introduction

Redwood Creek is located in Marin County, about ten miles north of San Francisco. It originates at an altitude of some 2,000 feet on the southern slopes of Mount Tamalpais, and wanders through Mount Tamalpais State Park and Muir Woods National Monument to Muir Beach and the open sea.

Redwood belongs to a small watershed—no more than a smudge of your fingertip on the map—with a drainage area of only about eight square miles. Yet this waterbody is alive with flora and fauna, parts of an intricate, functioning whole. The National Park Service recognizes the Redwood Creek watershed as a special ecological area, one that supports a high diversity of life within the folds of its ecosystem.

Coastal northern California's climate is typically Mediterranean, with blue-dry summers laced with fog and winters thick and gray with rain. But the day-to-day summer weather patterns along Redwood Creek have their own moods, often unique and distinct from the rest of the Bay Area. The Muir Woods microclimate is a blend of shade and moving air suffused with mists that blur forest spaces like cool muslin and feed the redwoods much of the water they need. This extra moisture keeps summer temperatures in Redwood Creek cool enough to support life.

Stretches of water sound out their stories in tune with the length of days, with the rise and fall of light. We can glimpse bits of these stories by coexisting with them for a while, discovering their colors. This work represents my record of those colors, "snapshots" of field work, inspirations, and a growing awareness of life in Redwood Creek, where I began surveys for the National Park Service in the summer of 1995.

The surface of Redwood Creek is often half-hidden, shrouded by shadows that fall like dark silk across its face. Exposed roots on the edge of the stream banks are strange and dark, giant bones. Patches of sun wash the rocky bottoms of shallows, and leaves twirl past in slow motion, like lost feathers. Viewed from the surface, Redwood Creek is shaded by the dense canopy that lines both sides of the water. In the canopy's gaps, the light falls through, turning the waters crystal green.

Viewed from underwater, Redwood's creekscape is uniquely beautiful. In the cool, smoky light, a small frill of overhanging ferns is a dense curtain of glassy jade, drawn down like blinds. Light tapers through the water in long, gold-green ribbons. The deep recesses of a cavern are mysterious, and straight ahead, a mixed school of coho salmon and steelhead trout thicken into shapes out of the blur.

Redwood Creek is home to a wide variety of fauna, including scarce species like the threatened coho salmon; steelhead trout, which has been proposed for endangered status; and the western pond turtle, listed as a species of concern. Abundant schools of native threespine stickleback dwell in its folds, and riffle sculpin skulk at the bottom of faster waters.

Each part of Redwood Creek, living or dead, is a prop or player in the drama of aquatic and riparian life. Giant logs are viewing terraces in a turtle's world. Networks of force connect living caddisflies to slight changes in temperature, affecting their movement and activities. Stretches of water, light, and heat carve lands slowly in geologic time, rapidly during floods. Creeks are in constant conversation with themselves, shaping their own slopes, edges, and moss-shaggy rocks.

Studies of this system have been carried out over the years by biologists and naturalists from University of San Francisco and San Jose State University, and by independent naturalists. During the summer, fall, and winter of 1995, Golden Gate National Recreation Area aquatic biologist Darren Fong organized an extensive series of new Redwood Creek surveys. Designed with the intention of using the results to develop conservation efforts that will ensure the future protection of the creek, they are ongoing.

One of the projects investigated the importance of creek habitat: the role of shape and shade and other structural features in supporting aquatic life. Parallel studies included counts of migrating adult and juvenile *salmonids* (fish belonging to the family Salmonidae, such as steelhead trout and coho salmon) for long stretches of the creek. These studies brought many people—including me—in close communion with this dynamic waterbody.

ABOUT THIS STORY

For days, we stood in the creek in our waders with our meter rods, the water tight around our knees, sinking into the soft silt. Then one morning, I found myself once more at the waterline measuring a stone with a six-inch ruler. I looked up and was suddenly filled with the vibrancy of this place: the shifting colors, birds flashing through the understory, stinging nettles a little too close to my face. My ruler seemed absurdly out of context and I thought, *I've got to go beyond this number-dry vision.*

With Darren's help, I started making notes to myself about the relevance of our work. At first I was immersed in the thick of dry ecological language (numbers, estimates, percentages). As time went on, I felt the need to translate this language into a more fluid one, and long hours spent creekside offered that translation.

Don't get me wrong—there is an undeniable benefit in numbers and measurements. They are used to develop estimates of habitat quality, of abundance in fish per stretch of water. Yet beyond the numbers, I felt an intrinsic appreciation for the living systems and natural processes I was helping monitor in Redwood Creek. This sort of feeling goes beyond the poise and elegance of estimates and numbers, and can be felt in the writings of Wendell Berry, Aldo Leopold, and Annie Dillard, among others.

This book aims to get at two worlds, linking ours to that of nature. I felt that none of our measurements had any importance unless they were included in the context of a deeper appreciation of the creek in all its complex processes. Perhaps these notes will catch the eye of some, drawing them closer to the creek and toward a compassion for this wild and tiny body of water, always thirsty for movement and song.

One

A FRAGILE HABITAT
Shadowy fish move through the clear water. Chiseled by birds, silence echoes among some of the tallest trees in the world, the coast redwood. The morning sun warms the air, and walkers and hikers line the quiet trails, enjoying the peaceful space, the gift of time in Muir Woods.

Redwood Creek is soil for the thousands of salmon seeds sown every year. Yet less than 5 percent will live to make it back to this waterbody that is their birthplace. These fish lead lives full of risk—indeed, humans are one of their dangers. Creek life is extremely vulnerable to disturbances, and Redwood Creek's small size magnifies that vulnerability.

Human-caused disturbances have had an effect on open spaces throughout the world. Muir Woods is part of the Golden Gate National Recreation Area, and in GGNRA alone, there are more than twenty-seven endangered species. Unfortunately, the list is growing. Throughout the park, work is being done to protect and restore the remaining habitat of these species.

Redwood Creek salmon are part of the population's southern range, and in most of its southern range, the coho have declined severely. For its coho salmon and steelhead trout, Redwood Creek is key to survival. One of the unique aspects of wild coho salmon is that each northern California population belongs to a distinct and unique gene pool. Once the fish from a specific population are gone, that is really the end of that particular genetic strain, even if cohos can still be found in other watersheds. This means that fish from each creek need to be protected.

In 1994, the Department of Fish and Game submitted a petition to list the coho salmon as a sensitive species; in October 1996, they were officially listed as threatened. (Steelhead trout have also been petitioned, and may be listed soon.) Because the slim populations could no longer sustain themselves in some California drainages, hatchery coho salmon were placed in creeks that had lost their native cohos.

Overall, Marin County has lost more than half of its coho salmon population, probably due to human activities such as dam building, changing of watercourses, bridge building, and agriculture. These activities, in turn, can cause pollution, erosion, and overall habitat degredation.

Lower Redwood Creek suffers from a number of problems. Runoff from seasonal rains carries polluting fecal waste from nearby grazing lands into the creek. Silt and mud are deposited along lower watershed areas, and the encroachment of roads, bridges, and parking areas on the stream and floodplain causes unnatural flooding. Over time, the flow capacity of these disturbed waters declines, which exerts pressure on the banks and reshapes the creek into a wider, more spread-out body of water.

Threats to Redwood Creek Life

Scientists believe that long-term declines of coho salmon populations parallel the extent of human-caused habitat deterioration. The home stream's year-round water quality is an extremely important factor in the survival and successful return of these fish; it doesn't take a lot of disturbance to affect them. Pollutants can damage gills and other delicate tissues—salmon have been known to lose the urge to move downward to the sea as a result of exposure to copper in the freshwater home. Detergents too can interfere with their sense of smell, as can something as seemingly innocuous as a person washing his or her hands in the creek's waters.

In the Redwood Creek watershed, waste-water disposal, water diversions, and creek bank alterations, e.g., straightening the creek throughout Muir Woods, are probably responsible for declines in fish populations. In addition, natural factors, such as El Niño effects, can have a dramatic impact.

Restoration itself often affects freshwater life; in the short term, native flora and fauna can experience consequences of work done to protect them. This is likely to be the case for Big Lagoon at Muir Beach, for which restoration plans are currently being developed. In the past, this lagoon was almost entirely filled in by silt and other runoff from nearby farming. Deepening this section of lower Redwood Creek by some ten feet, removing non-native vegetation, and recreating the lagoon's historic boundaries are some of the activities proposed for its restoration.

While lower Redwood Creek has felt the impact of agricultural and suburban activities, an impact that is reflected in its shape and condition, upper Redwood Creek remains relatively pristine; the diversity of aquatic insects that live there reflects its undisturbed conditions.

Animal mysteries are locked to their needs. Like other sensitive creek fauna, both coho and steelhead have specific habitat requirements that represent a fine balance of natural ingredients. Returning adults need a clean *substrate* (material on the creek bed) of gravel and cobble to dig out their *redds* (nests). These redds must be rinsed with fresh, dissolved oxygen to ensure easy breathing for the eggs nestling under swift winter flows. Once hatched, the young fish require quiet, cool pools where they can feed on insects carried to them by a slow swirl of current. Healthy flora and fauna are indicative of a healthy system, and the National Park Service is interested in discovering exactly how Redwood Creek and its watershed are faring.

It had been some time since Redwood Creek was first recognized and studied carefully as an important part of National Park Service lands. "In 1981," NPS Ranger Mia Monroe says, "park people were getting together on surveys that spanned many resource-related disciplines. Judd Howell coordinated this decentralized approach to learning how to manage local resources. I volunteered to be on the aquatics team, which was instructed by local legends like fisheries biologists Bill Cox and Willis Evans. We focused our attention on Redwood Creek because of its value as a free-flowing stream supporting coho salmon and steelhead trout runs. At the time, there were many knowledge gaps and no unified approach to management of these resources."

National Park Service philosophy has come a long way in its thinking about the Redwood Creek watershed, and management practices have changed since the 1981 surveys. Woody debris (dead and decaying wood in the creek), once removed from the creek for aesthetic reasons, is now recognized as an important habitat factor. Watershed management plans are being drawn up, and riparian vegetation is being restored to a more natural version of itself. For example, the banks of Fern Creek had been heavily eroded by foot traffic. In 1996, the National Park Service fenced and revegetated them and returned woody debris to the creek itself. This work was accomplished with a grant from the state's Wildlife Conservation Board. And each year on Earth Day, hundreds of volunteers line up to plant native riparian vegetation in and around the creek and to restore the habitat of the area. These efforts are directed in part by the answers to questions posed by the ongoing surveys.

THE QUESTIONS

Recent Redwood Creek surveys fit into the larger picture of efforts to preserve its mystery. In the 1995-1996 habitat study, we attempted to answer several important questions, including: How well does Redwood Creek habitat support sensitive fauna? Is there a healthy *riparian* (creekside) corridor with plants that provide shade and organic matter to the creek system? What is the diversity and abundance of aquatic *invertebrates* (insects) that support the life in Redwood Creek? What other factors contribute to the survival of young salmon until they depart for the sea? And of course, how many adult salmon make it up the stream?

The surveys also attempted to monitor numbers of adults and redds and the growth and numbers of young salmon to estimate spawning success. Because every inch of the watershed is shaped by the flora and fauna that support it, the focus of all of the projects was to link what was measured in the creek to the long-term survival success of these fish.

In 1995, a one-day survey of the entire Redwood Creek system turned up only about twenty-five returning adult salmon. On the other hand, during the same season, salmon surveys in Olema Creek (about twenty miles northwest), yielded a count of over two hundred adult salmon.

In *Muir Woods: Redwood Refuge*, author John Hart poses the question "Is Redwood Creek a good stream for salmon and trout?" and answers it. "If you compare it with other modern streams, the answer is: Yes, this habitat is excellent. If you compare it with what it once was and what it could be, the answer is: Not yet." Long-time Bay Area resident John O'Connor's recollection supports Hart's assessment—O'Connor recalls years when, during migration season, adult fish were "so thick you could barely see the water." The desire to help restore a natural balance and once again see Redwood Creek thick with adult fish is part of what drives the study of this vital creek and its watershed.

Two

THE WATERSHED Redwood Creek winds narrowly down through Muir Woods, its waterline etched by years of movement. Close to its headwaters, the small creek gushes with an intense power, straight and steep. Cascades slip over rocks and boulders, gathering in deep pool waters flashing with life. Thin streaks of shifting sun slice the water, and a fine spray fills the air.

The Redwood Creek watershed is a giant web of water—imagine each separate creek as filament of the web. Basically, a watershed is a huge wavy bowl made of hills and of canyons whose floors are the creeks' paths. Invisible threads of water flow from underground aquifers, collecting in Redwood Creek and its tributaries. These liquid strands knit together into one major creek. Eventually, they exhaust their freshwater energies across a blue beach and into the sea.

If you were to walk the circumference of the Redwood Creek watershed, you would start at the creek's mouth at Muir Beach, then head up to the top of a ridge (perhaps the ridge-top section of the Dipsea Trail). Walking up the ridge, you would see all the mini-creeks—such as Kent and Green Gulch—that belong to the Redwood Creek drainage family. You would continue walking up to the highest point of the watershed, Mount Tamalpais, where you would find the headwaters of the creek and its tributaries. To complete the circumference, you would walk along a ridge on the southern slopes of Mount Tam on the other side of the creek, down and back towards the sea. It would be quite a trip.

The creek changes dramatically as it approaches Muir Woods National Monument, becoming flatter and wider and running more gently than before. Cascades quiet into riffles and flatwater areas, and pools become calm (although there is one dramatic cascade that runs along the border of the Muir Woods parking lot). Close over the creek, a dome of riparian vegetation creates a fluid corridor of leaves, filled with stirring air. In its home stretch of flow to the sea, Redwood Creek slows through the Pacific Way Road section of Mount Tamalpais State Park and widens in its last twists towards the Pacific Ocean at Muir Beach.

REACHES: RIFFLES, POOLS, CASCADES, AND FLATWATER

Habitat *reaches* (segments) include riffles, pools, cascades, and flatwater. These types of reaches alternate throughout the creek's length, each serving as an important element of the creek habitat.

Fast-flowing turbulent reaches within creeks are called riffles. Riffles are certainly the most musical parts of Redwood Creek, a string quartet springing from rushing water, wound by some endless internal clock. Listen for them as you approach a creek. A small slope in a stretch of water causes this rushing, but riffles are usually not very deep—some of the shorter riffles in Redwood Creek have an average summer depth of barely five centimeters (about two inches). This bounce of water over cobble, gravel, and boulder dissolves oxygen into the creek. The riffles' drive also cleanses the water of silt and other fine particles that can clog the flow. Riffles support creek life, acting as spawning grounds for adult salmonids and as cover for their eggs and sometimes even *fry* (young fish). Dense communities of invertebrates can be found in riffle areas, and fish feed on the steady drift of insects that pour from them into the pools.

Pools are areas of deep, slow-moving water, usually with silty or sandy bottoms. Here, young salmonids school together in large numbers, foraging on insects. Three types of pools were identified in Redwood Creek: midchannel, scour, and backwater. Midchannel pools occur in the middle of the creek; these generally U-shaped pools tend to occur where the creek is its deepest. Scour pools are dug by fast water bouncing off unyielding boulders or large woody debris that has fallen into the stream; a twist in the stream when a riffle ends at a meander can carve out a scour pool. Scour pools tend to be shaped like a crooked U in cross-section. Backwater pools have been cut off from the main flow by a berm, and may be over a meter, or about 40 inches, deep. The flow of water in these pools is extremely slow, and sometimes eddies backwards. You can find such eddies by dropping a dry leaf into the current; if it circles around and goes back upstream, you're witnessing the effect of a backwater pool.

Lower Redwood Creek has numerous backwater pools—a particularly large backwater area at Muir Beach is accessible by a pedestrian bridge. Flanked on one side by a horse pasture and on the other by a narrow bank, it is separated from the main stem of Redwood Creek. Deep standing water reaches like this are good for the rarely seen western pond turtles, which have been observed here on sunny days, basking on logs.

Cascades are tumbling waters that either fall from a height, like a waterfall, or gradually, down steps of stones. Cascades are not very common in lower Redwood Creek—only two cascades are found between Muir Woods and Muir Beach. These plunging waters often scour out deep pools, and the nearby creek bottom is mostly large cobble and boulders. The water's speed and energy slices through time, smoothing down the boulders. A good, although human-made, example of a cascade can be found where Redwood Creek runs next to the Muir Woods parking lot. The boulders that form the cascade were put there in the 1930s as part of an effort to build a wall along the left bank of the creek. In the five-foot drop between the beginning and end of this short cascade, the waters churn fast, playing loop and harp on the massive sleeping rocks.

Flatwater is a gliding stretch of water with a generally steady flow. It is slower and deeper than a riffle, and without turbulence. The creek bottom of a flatwater area often has an almost identical substrate size as a riffle area, but because the water flows slower in flatwaters than in riffles, there tends to be more silt. Flatwater stretches, often sandwiched between a riffle and a pool, are very common in Redwood Creek. Flatwater areas with good cover—big boulders or overhanging plants—provide excellent fish habitat.

THE INSECT WORLD

Numerous types of aquatic invertebrates are salmon food, and are abundant in Redwood Creek. Many drift down with the water current, to be snatched up by juvenile fish waiting downstream. The diversity of a stream's insect world is a reflection of the watercourse's health. The Environmental Protection Agency interprets the presence of a variety of stoneflies, mayflies, and caddisflies (case builders) as an indicator of good water quality, and Redwood Creek has them all.

Insect types vary from reach to reach; diversity is linked closely to elements such as flow, riparian vegetation, and woody debris. For example, some varieties of dragonflies and damselflies tend to be found in slower pools and backwater areas, while most stoneflies are found in fast-water reaches. Flatwater and pools are also home to a non-native crayfish, a relatively large and aggressive invertebrate with colorful blue-and-red claws.

Many invertebrates move from water into air in ways that are just as dramatic as the salmons' freshwater-to-saltwater migration. Dragonflies, mayflies, and stoneflies exist in water during the earliest stages of their

Water Striders

Stonefly Larva

Water Boatman

Ripple Beetle

Back-swimmer

Riffle Beetle

Mayfly Larva

18

lives, then leave the water for the air, where they fly, mate, and die as adults. As eggs, larvae, and pupae, they are adapted for a waterlogged life. Their gills, exoskeletons, or heavy cases made of pebbles are shed once they become terrestrial. Some stoneflies are especially sensitive to reduced oxygen levels; they have no gills and oxygen exchange takes place through their skin.

Temperature and the length of the days are the clocks of insect time. Once their life in water is over, generally in the full swing of summer, they crawl up onto a rock or log. This requires quite an effort, one made against moving surface water. Some insects take a break after *ecdysis* (shedding their shell). Motionless, they wait for their bodies and soft wings to harden. Then they are ready to speak the language of air and fly away as adults.

Before they die, female aquatic insects return to water to lay their eggs. The shallow edge of a midchannel pool in Muir Woods was the site chosen by a black-and-yellow dragonfly. She stopped short of the water's surface, hovering. Not looking, she lowered herself tail-first past the seam of water, into the mud, then bobbed up and then

mayfly

Water Strider

Damselfly

Riffle Beetle

Caddisfly larva

Dobsonfly larva

Caddisfly larva

midgefly larva

down close by. She stitch-stitched her way back and forth across the pool, hovering over the thick, protective cloth of silt, laying her eggs.

Locked into each egg were embryos and globes of yolk to feed them through a season until they awoke and could fatten in the water. Still later, they would crawl ashore and let the air take them, wings hardening into veined, dry scales. Now water, that green crystal, held them still.

Simple observations of invertebrates were made by looking closely at the creek bottom. Counting pebbles in the habitat surveys often revealed a piece of cobble crawling with tiny mayflies, impatient to be returned to the water. A close look at gravel and cobble-rich areas revealed caddisfly cases attached to the tops or sides of stones.

A stonefly exoskeleton on a log jam provided an instructive example of insect anatomy. From face to claw, the exoskeleton was identical to the original larva that once lived inside it. Stoneflies are robust invertebrates, some more than half an inch long, which is large for an aquatic insect in Redwood Creek. They have two claws on each of their six legs, and they have two tail-like *cerci* (appendages serving as tactile organs) to help them swim. Dictated by an internal clock, the dorsal part of the exoskeleton had unzipped perfectly straight and released the winged adult from its cage.

Shaped by the Seasons

Seasons knit a variety of shapes into Redwood Creek, and rain is the wool that feeds these weavings of water. Flood and drought, live and dead vegetation mark creek time, clicking like a pulse. During the dry summer, water levels sink and Redwood Creek slows to a modest fraction of itself; toward the latter half of the summer, the water inches closer and slower over the stony creekbed, and it is hard to imagine that full-grown salmon can return to these delicate liquid threads.

In drought years, the flow may stop in some reaches. Luckily, there are deep pools where the fauna can thrive even with no flows. This patchwork of small pools perseveres, studded with isolated fragments of creek life. In good rain years, Redwood Creek flows last through the summer, even though they slacken to their all-time annual low by fall.

Finally, winter rains sweep through like loud music and the water levels rise and vastly change Redwood's creekscape. Each year, the speeding flood waters carve banks and beds into shapes that will stay at least until the next wet season. On December 4, 1995, for example, in one long spate of rains, creek levels rose by four feet overnight! Other tributaries, such as Fern Creek (located between Bridge 3 and Bridge 4 in Muir Woods) and tiny Kent Creek (further down in Kent Canyon), were gushing in full flow, pouring their cloudy waters into Redwood. Downstream, the creek swept out in a frenzy toward the sea. Dark cumulus clouds hung low over equally dark waters. Invisible teeth of wind whipped the beach's gulls into a swirling mass. Back in Muir Woods, the creek roared, a strong, syrupy river. Silt was pulled off the creek banks; suspended solids, a measure of the amount of silt, can be twenty times higher in the winter than during summer flows.

These flood-high flows last only a few hours, dropping rapidly as soon as the rains end. The water marks where it wipes the soil, often leaving webs of dead leaves in small hollows. When the water runs low again, a virtual road map of the flood times can be seen in the patterns of bank erosion.

Vegetation and woody debris also have a lot to do with the shape of the creek, especially lower Redwood Creek. During storms, debris is swept down to the lower, wider reaches, where it collects and influences the strength of water flow around it. The water-swept debris that collects in complexes, dams, and jams also helps carve deeper reaches. Hidden from the light, young fish nestle in the watery caves created by debris and boulders or cobble, places where the slow flow and cool light fill their days.

Spring and early summer are bustling times for life in the creek. Coho salmon and steelhead trout transform from eggs to little fry. Invertebrates grow thick among riffle stones, chewing up leaf litter and algae as they mature toward flight. Into this busy world, armed with ruler, pen, and waterproof paper, surveyors march creekward, determined to uncover the secrets of life in Redwood Creek.

Three

THINKING LIKE A FISH A single dead redwood has fallen across the creek, creating thousands of shadows. The inside is clean and hollowed out. Old and moss-shagged, it has been here awhile. Inside the meter-wide hollow, stones lie as neat and poised as though someone had arranged them.

A shaft of light cuts straight through the water—at certain times of the day, the entire hollow is suffused with a thick glow. In a flood, this place would be an ideal rest stop for salmon and steelhead. Filled to the brim with water, it is stillness in a rushing world.

Overhanging vegetation, cool water temperature, tree shade, and undercut banks are critical to the health of the creek. Habitat measurements explore these facets and demonstrate the creek's suitability for aquatic organisms. Measurements include invertebrate sampling to determine whether enough food is available, and calculating water flow changes to find how much summer dryness slows down the creek. According to park aquatic biologist Darren Fong, making these measurements requires one to "think like a fish." It also involves dividing the stream into segments and then wading carefully through each one, making observations about flow, depth, and substrate. There is counting to be done as well: width of trunk, total amount of close cover, and size of stones. Once each habitat unit is named and quantified, various elements of the unit are estimated. Making these estimates reinforces respect for the creek and its intricacies.

TEMPERATURE

Water and temperature are intimately linked in summer's annual cycle of sharp sun, trickle-low flows, and creek health. Summer water temperatures above 77 degrees Fahrenheit are lethal to young steelhead and coho. Insects that spend part of their lives in water depend on an increase in temperature to tell them when it is time to leave; even an unseasonable two-degree rise can cause aquatic insects to emerge too early from a cool stream. Destruction of riparian vegetation can result in these critical upward shifts in daytime temperatures in a slow pool.

High temperatures are unhealthy for aquatic fauna in another way as well, as heat depletes the water's oxygen level. Dissolved oxygen is what the creek's life breathes, and low levels can weaken or kill creek dwellers.

OXYGEN AND SHADE

The movement of water captures oxygen from the air, trapping it as carbon dioxide is trapped inside soda. Levels of oxygen vary from area to area of the creek. In active waters, turbulence creates many oxygen bubbles. Where water is slow and rotting algae is present, oxygen levels can be low. Studies have shown that when the level of dissolved oxygen is low, salmonids are hampered in their ability to process and throw off toxic wastes such as ammonia.

Shade also has an important bearing on how the fish will do in a particular reach. Warm, slow-moving stretches, areas without tree cover, often have high levels of algae enriched into abundance by direct sunlight and gentle water flow. When algae dies and rots, it uses up a substantial amount of the creek's dissolved oxygen. Fortunately, Redwood Creek has very few areas that have been unnaturally deprived of tree cover. Shade usually means lower temperatures and thus less algae growth, which is important to the maintenance of a good fish habitat.

Riparian Vegetation

Riparian vegetation is part of a creek's life-support system and directly affects the composition of its population. It includes all plants naturally found on the sides of a water resource. In the Redwood Creek watershed, a dense canopy of alders, arroyo willows, and yellow willows, and an understory of nettles, thimbleberrys, lady ferns, and native morning glories shade and enrich the creek's banks.

"Overhang" is defined as all vegetation or other cover that falls a foot or less over the water's surface; dense creekside ferns are a good example. Close to the creek, these ferns, trees, and other plants tilt into the water and this creates good cover for fish.

Riparian vegetation is richer and fatter with water than that found on dry hillsides. Plant roots drink soil water, using their long straw of xylem cells to transport the water to their leaves. This wet vegetation burns less readily than that in drier areas. (During the 1995 "Vision Fire" at Point Reyes National Seashore, some riparian vegetation in many areas of the fire's path seemed to maintain its green foliage.)

The riparian zone performs other functions vital to the health of a living watershed. In Redwood Creek, it serves as a floodplain, dissipating the energies associated with high flow. Tree roots stabilize creek banks and prevent excessive erosion problems during floods and heavy rain, and undercut banks house a multitude of fauna in their close protection.

Riparian vegetation also provides the organic matter that feeds creek-dwelling insects, which in turn feed the fish. Dense invertebrate communities are often found in areas with heavy vegetation.

UNDERCUT

Undercut is water and time working together: minutes, years, eons biting at the sides of the creek bank, breaking it down, flooding it, chewing off the silt. Meanwhile, the root-grip remains, creating a grotto. It can be a quiet space with slow flow, pulsing with steelhead and coho. It is a place where light bounces off and shadows spill in, cleaning the space, calming it. Undercut is a soft place, where scour hollows time.

WOODY DEBRIS

Wood is stored energy, the sun captured by leaves swallowing its light. Woody debris provides a tough and well-weathered frame for a diversity of aquatic life forms. Unlike leaves that are quickly softened and changed by water, wood is hardy.

In Redwood Creek, winter flood flows carry fallen trees into the waterbody, and these often dramatically alter the channel, deepening and slowing it down. Log jams make enormous natural dams in the creek, and high waters toss over them. These fast waters in turn carve deep hollows, digging at the floor of the creek. From the water's edge, log jams may look a mess, but underwater, they provide spacious, protected caverns. This series of safe havens, places where light is broken into ribbons, provides good cover from both sun and predators. Fish *thermoregulate* (control the temperature of their bodies) in the heat of the summer months by taking refuge under the cover of woody debris or boulders. One of the recent surveys indicated that if young salmon have access to adequate woody debris, they can coexist in higher numbers.

ORGANIC DEBRIS

Organic debris, vital to the sustenance of invertebrate life, is quite a challenge to measure. It includes leaf litter, rotting wood, and plant

Fines   Gravel   Small Cobble

matter that happens into the creek by flood or breeze. This debris thickens and softens the creek bottom, making life possible for a bustling array of invertebrates in this tugging, circling world. They chew it, live inside it, and hide in it; cased caddisflies, for example, build mobile homes out of tiny twigs, and crawl around protected by these little "shells."

This organic material represents the starting point for energy arrows that move upward through the system: consumed by insects that will be eaten by a fish that may eventually be devoured in a single gulp by a seabird.

Substrate

In creeks, a substrate is a solid surface anywhere within a body of water. It includes all shapes and sizes of stones, wood, and leaves and is a hardwood or rocky floor for the bugs and salamanders that slip through its crevices. Substrate is also a home garden patch for the scrapers and leaf-chewers among the aquatic fauna. (See page 55 for a

Large Cobble

Boulder

29

quantification of Redwood Creek substrate.)

In Redwood Creek, the substrate changes from boulders, large cobble, and gravel to fine silt that stirs into slow brown clouds when disturbed. Although substrate varies widely over the course of the creek, a pattern emerges as one moves downstream. Upper Redwood's substrate is made up primarily of large boulders, cobble, and gravel, with little silt and fines. The amount of fines increases as the creek gets closer and closer to the ocean.

As days shorten and temperatures drop, cold winter flows wash across Redwood Creek's substrate. Swelled with rain and smelling of home, the creekbed waits for the sound of slapping tails.

Four

THE GREAT MIGRATION *It is twilight and the light is fading fast. In a shallow riffle area, the water is sharp and clear as an evening star and the salmon pair is still easily visible. The male visits the female briefly, his chest and hooked mouth speeding toward her, his body curling around her seeds.*

Then in a flash of smoky red, he is gone. The female stays close to her nest, fanning it with her tail. She is too exhausted to notice that she is being watched. Fine bones show through her torn tail and dorsal fins, and her eye looks quite blind. Her body twists sideways and once more she slaps the water, cleaning the silt from her gravel-held eggs.

Each winter, mature adult salmon undertake an arduous journey from the open Pacific Ocean to the tiny upper pockets of Redwood Creek. Fish migrating back to smaller creeks like Redwood are called "short-run" salmon. The four- to five-inch-long yearlings that swam to the ocean about three years earlier are now twenty-two to twenty-eight inches long and weigh as much as ten pounds.

A combination of short days and cool temperatures probably cues their instinct to find and move up the creek in which they were born. At sea, migration routes may be guided by magnetic forces and light; much remains unknown about the inner pulse that guides their saltwater paths.

In the ocean, adult salmon face numerous threats. For those that do survive, the journey back to their creek is a treacherous one—evolution has taught predators about salmon time. It is also demanding, one that requires them to change their very blood to accommodate a vastly different environment. A salmon's journey between the saltwater and freshwater realms is as drastic as a trip from the Arctic to the Sahara.

When the time to migrate comes, salmon completely stop feeding; they will depend on largely their own tissues to nourish them. Egg- and sperm-making energy needs are high—food and even the fishs' digestive organs and parts of their muscles are absorbed back into their systems. Scientists have noted spawning coho salmon with no visceral organs other than hearts and kidneys, which pumped just enough fluids through them to keep them alive.

On reaching their native home, they must wait for entry. For part of the year, Redwood Creek is blocked by a sandbar at Muir Beach that separates its fresh waters from the salty Pacific. Migrating fish wait for heavy winter rains to open this door, and waiting in the sea is not safe. Eventually, though, cold fingers of rain slip in and take down the bar like a sandcastle dissolving in high tide.

Fresh water flows into the sea and the migrants smell their creek.

Depending on the rains, coho start the journey up Redwood Creek between late November and February, with peak numbers generally occurring in December. Steelhead trout arrive at the creek a little later, usually in January, and their numbers slow by late March.

Muscles tuned for opposing flows, the salmon migrate upstream by night, flashing their dorsal fins in the dark translucence of fast waters. They navigate up short cascades; some, provided a thin, uninterrupted film of water, can swim vertically upward through a fall. In general, steelhead are stronger swimmers and make it to higher reaches. In Cheda Creek, a tributary of Olema Creek near the town of Olema at Point Reyes National Seashore, the steelhead have been able to get past a culvert, but no coho have been found past this point. (The steelhead are strong leapers!)

SCENT OF A STREAM

Much about salmon migration remains unknown, but it is thought that they use an acute sense of smell to recognize their native stream. Humans have a sharp sense of smell, but after repeated exposure to an odor, tend to become less aware of it. A salmon's olfactory sense, however, remains sensitive and strong. These animals can detect water-borne concentrations as small as fifty parts per billion. "In martini equivalents," says writer Tom Jay, "they can detect roughly one drop of vermouth in 500,000 barrels of gin."

As noted earlier, each creek has a smell unique to it alone—soil and plants impart their special odors. Depending on the season, the waters of Redwood Creek may smell of softened redwood needles and leaves of willow, oak, and alder, peppered with loose silt. Plants like red alder are common around Redwood Creek, and chemicals specific to their leaves dissolve over time. These tiny molecules become part of the beacon that guides adult salmon back home.

Early studies showed that salmon could be induced to swim up the wrong stream by introducing a chemical into their native stream and then reintroducing it into a different one years later, when these individuals were ready to migrate back to their home waters. In nature, however, only about 5 percent of migrating salmon make a mistake and go up the wrong creek. Normally, this happens in creeks that are in close proximity; those separated by many miles have different combinations of soil and vegetation, and so are not randomly strayed into. Straying can be good news, as it leads to a healthy cross-breeding between salmon populations. Unfortunately, there are no longer any creeks close to the

Redwood Creek watershed, so its small existing populations are alone and fragile.

SPAWNING, BIRTH, AND DEATH

On reaching Redwood Creek, the salmon swim up toward the higher reaches, close to the headwaters above Muir Woods. Some swim up the tributaries—Fern Creek and Kent Creek each have small salmon populations. On their way, they pause to rest in pools and slow-flowing waters. At last they stop in the creek's fast-moving reaches. The female salmon chooses an area of clean gravel and cobble, usually found at the tails of pools where water picks up speed and turns into a riffle. She will also select flatwater areas as nesting sites. The male fertilizes the eggs laid by the female, and she covers them with clean substrate.

The amount of fines in the substrate is inversely proportional to hatching success. If the eggs are buried under cloudy fines during late-season floods, the salmons' breeding efforts will be unsuccessful. Fines slow the flow of water across the eggs, reducing the supply of oxygen available to them. In extreme situations, fines-covered eggs can become *anoxic* (without oxygen) very quickly, and this condition can kill them.

Fanning the nest with her whole body, she slaps at the creek bottom to clean the gravel of silt and sediment. She will lay about a hundred eggs in each nest; for protection, the eggs are deposited about six inches below the level of the substrate. She continues to move upstream, building redds and laying eggs that trailing males then fertilize along the way. Over the course of the spawning period, the female lays about 3,500 eggs, almost all of which are fertilized by an attendant male.

About the fifth day of the spawning process, the female loosens her hold on the current and lets the swell carry her down, gills still clicking weakly. Eventually, both she and the male die, their bodies feeding the stream with nutrients, such as nitrogen and phosphates, that are then pulled up by water plants. Meanwhile, her eggs sleep, clinging to their pebble nest through a long gushing winter of high flows. They will hatch, swollen with yolk, food from their parents for their first days alive. When they've absorbed the yolk, they will emerge as fry, flickering like small fireworks in the spring light.

A NEW GENERATION

"The eggs can see," wrote Tom Jay. "They have eyes." At first they are seeds, knots of life, clinging to their gravel womb. Then in the spring, coho eggs hatch and the fry start to grow. Redwood Creek will be their home for at least a year. Steelhead trout may stay in the creek for two or even three years before migrating out to their saltwater domain, and can make several round trips, as they do not die after spawning.

Puffy stomachs rich and heavy with yolk, newly hatched fry look like tadpoles. They move little, remaining in their redds, soaking up the small treasury of yolk food. Once this is absorbed, they emerge from the gravel. During late spring and early summer, these young fish congregate on stream margins and in shallow pools and backwater eddies, gathering food. As warmth rises with the dawn, insects beat the water's surface and, tired, alight; they are swallowed whole.

As the young salmon (now known as parr) grow, they move into pools and become aggressive and territorial; both coho and steelhead prefer pools' low-velocity water, as it means that they do not have to spend all their energy fighting the currents. Facing upstream riffles, they feed on aquatic insects floating downstream with the drift. At dusk, the young fish shoot up through the skin of the water in sun-streaked pools where the waterstriders dance, then vanish again into the gray-green water depths.

Coho salmon can be distinguished from young steelhead trout by their long, graceful tiger stripes. They also have a pale, unspotted dorsal fin and large eyes. Steelhead have broad oval marks running down their sides, and their dorsal fins are covered with tiny black spots.

SMOLTIFICATION

Early summer sharpens the coho's fins to wingborn-edges ready for seaward flight. They are now about 100 millimeters (four inches) long. Right before they move down to the ocean, the young fish lose their

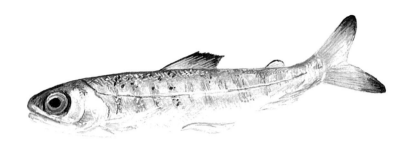

tiger-stripe markings and become silvery, like anchovies. They also gain a little in size; at this point, they are known as smolts.

Smolts are more buoyant than their younger counterparts, and this makes it easier for them to travel downstream. They also become less territorial and increasingly able to tolerate seawater, which would kill them during the parr stage. Most important, it is during the smolt period that salmon start imprinting, the process of memorizing their stream's smell. Salmon brains are imprinted with the particular odor of their native stream at between a year and three years old (steelhead imprinting generally happens when they are somewhat older). Their brains record an exact olfactory image of their freshwater home.

In the early spring and summer of 1996, Darren Fong and several volunteers set out to understand the salmons' downstream migration. During the survey, almost 5,000 salmon and steelhead were caught, counted, and released back into the stream. Surprisingly, most were not smolts but young under a year old, forced down by high flows.

Most downward movement took place during the night and into

the small hours of the morning. The numbers varied from day to day. Traps that captured only thirty fish one day held more than two hundred the next. They apparently schooled in the pools and then drifted down together. During the survey, the numbers shifted in sudden waves, as though a lunar alarm clock were going off.

While moving down the creek, smolts and juveniles face threats from hungry belted kingfishers and great blue herons, which have been observed stalking the waters from the tops of riparian vegetation or along shaded creekside spots.

Finally, a small percentage of the number that started out will once again reach the open sea; fewer than that will ultimately return to complete the cycle of life that their existance demands. And the measuring and counting continue.

Five

LOOKING IN LAYERS Spawning surveys begin on typical cold, gray Redwood Creek winter mornings. Creek walkers caught in a salmon spell wear river feet (hip waders). Some of the salmon hold their restless pace in deep pools, others slow down in shallows and riffles.

I almost step on the first salmon I see—she is fanning her torn tail in a dark shallow area in front of me. At first, she does not react, then she streaks upstream to the opposite bank.

In the summer, we kept track of the abundance of fish in certain well-lit reaches. Snorkeling was an excellent non-interfering way to view the fish in their daily biological rhythms, and provided us with a gold mine of information about fish behavior and habits.

Snorkeling Redwood Creek pools, I felt the water breathing around me. The creek's midchannel pool (Number 48) came alive with golds and greens. Straight in front of my gliding path, a school of fish thickened out of the blur. They quivered with the effort to steady themselves in the current. The sun rippled in long strands and the water fed each minute with its humming. I reached for a thick overhanging root, its bare tentacles spreading into the water. Hanging on to the root with one hand, I pulled myself ever-so-slightly closer to the fish. Their fluid formation instantly changed in the current I caused, and they drifted toward an undercut bank where the light tapered into darkness. Fish have lateral lines, a very special touch sense that makes them sensitive to water movements, breaks, or interruptions. Using these lateral lines, fish align themselves in perfect tune with water flow and with each other.

A couple of weeks later, I surveyed Kent Creek, a tiny tributary of Redwood that dries out over the course of the late summer months. There was a concern that the salmon stuck in isolated Kent Creek pools might not make it to the winter rainy season. I walked up the dry creek bed, sure that I would find nothing. Here and there, the power of a once-raging current was visible—leaf litter on the bank or woody debris washed to one side. Now, the banks of Kent Creek were a tangle of thick riparian scrub and ferns, and in some places the vegetation knotted low over the creek bed, which seemed to have forgotten that it was ever filled to overflowing with water. A stray cat and several warblers moved in the deep silence of the waterless creek. On my hands and knees, chin close to the ground, I picked up a dry pebble and turned it over. It was dark with a thin layer of moisture, and smelled of rain. I put the pebble back.

About a hundred yards from the place where a road crosses Kent Creek was a pool that was only about a meter (approximately three feet) across and a couple of meters long. When I dipped my snorkel-masked face in, I was surprised. A school of some twenty salmon hung there like lanterns in the dim shadows. Caddisflies lugged their heavy wood-chip cases around, and I watched as they moved freely below the salmon. Then a small worm wriggled into view, and a young coho scooped it up in one gulp, like spaghetti.

As I walked farther upstream, I found other pools like this one. Most were just as small and isolated, with no apparent flow of water between them—perhaps some hidden underground source kept them fresh. Yet schools of fish teemed in each one. I counted forty coho and steelhead in a deeper pool. A huge hollow tree trunk held part of another pool, and I found at least fifteen fish in there.

Far upstream near the headwaters, where the redwoods grow, I reached a cascade, home to two fully grown rainbow trout. These fish stay in creeks all their lives, never migrating downstream to the ocean. Other than size—the trout are smaller—and slight variations in color patterns, there are few visible differences between them and adult steelheads. One fish "hid" from view by playing camouflage: it flattened itself against a rocky depression and remained motionless, watching me.

As summer wears on, the exhausted scrub will lose leaves and provide less shade. Kent Creek's waters will absorb more sun and heat, and pool levels will become lower and oxygen thinner. Only the fish in the deepest pools will survive.

Long shafts of light angle straight through the shimmering leaves and shoot into the stream. The light enters the water and bends, looking thicker as it reaches the bottom. It shines on the stones at the bottom, and I think, *cobble, fines, silt, gravel.* Fins pulse in a current that hums low, like a stringed instrument played in tune over cobblestones. I remove the stones one by one, like pieces of a jigsaw puzzle, and take a stone reading: 25 centimeters (a little over nine inches) in width. I put each piece back carefully.

Wet knees and elbows follow the knots of root and light, places where time has printed a pattern. In the coolness of the late afternoon, the creek comes alive again. Fish slip straight and clear out of the water to catch insect snacks. They land with a smack and ripples bob in their wake. A dragonfly swoops down and hangs in mid-air, as though poised in thought. Other insects, high in the bright air, circle in a frenzy with what seems to be the last bit of energy left from a glorious day. Gloaming slips in, thin as satin.

Afterword

Late one afternoon, a rambling passer-by threw me a question: "Are you looking for gold in the creek?" he laughingly asked.

To which I replied: "It depends on what you think gold is. To me, the coho salmon are gold enough."

"So what are you doing?" he asked again, a little slower, a little more carefully this time.

And I answered in simple terms: "I am checking to see if the fish here have ample space to live the rest of their young existence here. And if the older ones have clean places to dig up their nests. . ."

The Redwood Creek surveys meant different things to those lucky enough to participate in them. As for me, I became acutely aware of the vulnerability of small waterbodies. In this place I revere greatly, I did my work quietly and left with minimum disturbance.

Muir Woods is is a place of true listening. Tiny discoveries make themselves visible if you give them time. Thousands of migrant ladybugs gather in sleepy clusters in the winter season. Spotted owls ruffle themselves so vigorously that they look as though they might lose their balance and fall off their perch. Fawns stray from their mothers' watchful eyes, nibbling at buds that frame Redwood Creek like small crowns. In the water, riffle sculpins hold still, their pectoral fins resembling two large, hand-held fans, pulsing with light. And of course, in the winter, during the last few days of their lives, salmon slap their bodies against the water's surface. (Olema Creek at Point Reyes is another place to observe winter salmon migrations and spawning; they come up this creek by the hundreds.)

Sit quietly and examine your surroundings. The colors of Redwood Creek can be seen by anyone who makes the effort. Amy Lambert, who has taught high school students an awareness of layers, comments, "I tell them to count all the greens they can spot, starting with the whitest green and ending with the blackest green. You'd be amazed at what they come up with. I can sit in a cascade along Bootjack Trail and count silver-green, lichen-green, stone-green, shadow-green. As long as I'm counting, new shades leap out at me."

Western Pond Turtle

There are many ways to join the conservation effort while you explore Muir Woods. Watch Redwood Creek only from the trails—fish are stressed very easily, and getting in the water can scare schools away. Another problem with stepping onto the banks is that the riparian vegetation often gets damaged in the process. For example, the banks in parts of Fern Creek have little riparian canopy remaining. Without this vegetation, they are easily swept away by winter floods, reducing or eliminating good habitat like undercut and pool depth. As mentioned earlier, the new riparian vegetation on Fern Creek's eroded banks is the result of recent restoration efforts.

How does the park talk about issues of habitat degradation and preservation to visitors? Muir Woods ranger Mia Monroe answered this question for me.

"Muir Woods is a fortunate platform to talk about those issues. You know, it's a beautiful setting, and it provokes good responses in people. We talk about the limits we might have to place on land use, about staying on trails, recycling garbage, even writing letters to legislators. I ask people 'When was the last time you watched an environmental news program instead of regular TV?' and 'Can you give Muir Woods a Saturday to help plant native vegetation?' I believe in letting people know what they can do instead of just saying, 'It's awful out there.' "

You can support and take part in creek and creekside activities by joining programs like Adopt-a-Creek or Muir Woods Earth Day. To find out about these and other restoration, monitoring, and protection projects in the Golden Gate National Recreation Area, call Muir Woods National Monument (415) 388-2596; the NPS aquatic ecologist (415) 331-8716; or the NPS Volunteer Coordinator (415) 556-3535.

To help financially or volunteer for habitat restoration programs, contact the Golden Gate National Parks Association at (415) 776-0693.

The Redwood Creek Riparian Environment

LIFE IN THE CREEK AND ALONG THE BANKS

Following is a selected list of the Redwood Creek riparian community. It is not exhaustive and should be considered only as a starting point for anyone wishing to learn more about the Redwood Creek watershed and its inhabitants.

Flora

TREES & SHRUBS

Arroyo willow, *Salix lasiolepis*; and yellow willow, *Salix lucida* ssp. *lasiandra*

Bay laurel, *Umbellularia californica*

Bigleaf maple, *Acer macrophyllum*

Blackberry, *Rubus ursinus*

Blue Elderberry, *Sambucus mexicana*

California buckeye, *Aesculus californica*

California coastal redwood, *Sequoia sempervirens.* Muir Woods National Monument was created to protect this magnificent redwood. In 1905, Marin County residents Elizabeth and William Kent purchased the redwood-filled canyon, and in 1908, donated it to the United States government.

Coast live oak, *Quercus agrifolia*

Douglas fir, *Pseudotsuga menziesii* var. *menziesii*

Red alder, *Alnus rubra*. A common stream-side tree, the red alder is a member of the birch family.

Toyon, *Heteromeles arbutifolia*

FERNS AND FORBS

Bog lupine, *Lupinus* ssp. Historically associated with Big Lagoon but not recently documented.

Bulrush, *Scirpus* ssp.

Elk clover, *Aralia californica*. Leaves can be as large as 5 by 7 inches. This plant is a member of the ginseng family and has small white clustered flowers that turn into purple berries in the fall.

Ferns, non-flowering plants that grow best in shady, moist areas.
Bracken, *Pteridium aquilinum* var. *pubescens*
Fivefingered, *Adiantum aleuticum*
Lady, *Athyrium felix-femina* var. *cyclosporum*

Horsetail, *Equisetum* spp. An ancient, primitive plant, even older than the redwood. Horsetails grow at the base of redwood trees, and their feathery branches (not leaves) contain silica, which made the plant ideal as a pioneer's cleaning tool.

Miner's lettuce, *Claytonia perfoliata*. Historically associated with Big Lagoon but not recently documented.

Morning glory, *Calystegia occidentalis*

Redwood sorrel, *Oxalis oregana*. Although it resembles clover, sorrel is actually one of several plants in a group with the non-scientific name "shamrock."

Redwood trillium (Western wake robin), *Trillium ovatum*

Redwood (Evergreen) violet, *Viola sempervirens*

Sticky monkeyflower, *Mimulus aurantiacus*. Historically associated with Big Lagoon but not recently documented.

Stinging nettle, *Urtica dioica* ssp. *gracilis* (*U. californica*)

Thimbleberry, *Rubus parviflorus*

Fauna

COMMON AQUATIC INVERTEBRATES

Blackfly, *Simulium* sp.

Caddisfly
    Case, *Lepidostoma* sp.
    Free-living, *Rhyacophilia* sp.
    Net-spinning, *Hydropsyche* sp.

Cranefly, *Dicranota* sp.

Elmid water beetle, *Narpus concolor, Optioservus quadrimaculatus, Ordobrevia* sp.

Mayfly, *Baetis* sp., *Praleptophlebia* sp., *Rhithrogena* sp.

Perlid stonefly, *Calineuria californica*

Water mite, *Hydracarina*

OTHER AQUATIC INVERTEBRATES

Back swimmer, Family Notonectidae

Damselfly, *Argia* sp.

Dobsonfly, *Neohermes* sp.

Dragonfly, *Anax* sp.

Riffle beetle, *Hydrophilus* sp.

Signal Crayfish, *Pacifasticus leniusculus*

Water boatman, Family Corixidae

Water strider, Family Gerridae

FISH

Coho salmon, *Oncorhynchus kisutch*; also called silver salmon; anadromous, which means that it begins its life in freshwater, migrates to saltwater, and then returns to freshwater to reproduce.

Rainbow trout, *Oncorhynchus mykiss* or *Salmo gairdnerii*; fresh-water game fish, named for the distinctive reddish band on its side.

Steelhead trout, *Oncorhynchus mykiss* or *Salmo gairdnerii*; anadromous, an ocean-going form of rainbow trout.

Threespine stickleback, *Gasterosteus aculeatus*, a slender green fish; the males build intricate suspended nests and guard the eggs and the young.

Riffle sculpin, *Cottus* sp. These small, bottom-dwelling fish feed on larvae and midges; they can be seen hanging motionless in the water, slightly above the substrate.

REPTILES & AMPHIBIANS

Pacific treefrog, *Hyla regilla*. Average size, 1 to 2 inches; black eye stripe and large toe pad; found among low plant growth near water.

Salamander

California newt, *Taricha torosa*. Breeds in slow-flow areas.

California slender, *Batrachoseps attenuatus*. Breeds in damp leaf litter.

Ensatina, *Ensatina eachscholtzii*

Pacific giant, *Dicamptodon ensatus*. Averages between 2.5 and
7 inches long, frequents damp forests in or near clear, cold streams.

Western pond turtle, *Clemmys marmorata*. A thoroughly aquatic turtle;
feeds on vegetation and invertebrates.

SUBSTRATE COMPOSITION

Following is the author's quantification of Redwood Creek's substrate (in
ascending size order); see pages 28-29 for illustration.

Fine and coarse organic debris
‹2 mm, or .08"	fines/smallest particles of sand (less than pinhead size)
2-64 mm, or 2.5"	gravel (between pea and lime size)
65-127 mm, or 5"	small cobble (to grapefruit size)
128-255 mm, or 10"	large cobble (to watermelon size)
›256 mm	boulder

GENERAL WATERSHED STATISTICS

Annual measurable precipitation, 40"

Number of days with fog, 140

Spring and summer water temperatures, 45 to 65 degrees F.

Rainy season, November through April

Rainfall required to open Muir Beach sandbar, 2 to 3 inches

Resources and References

GENERAL

Delp, Michael. *Under the Influence of Water*. Detroit, MI: Wayne State University Press, 1992.

Hart, John. *Muir Woods: Redwood Refuge*. San Francisco: Golden Gate National Parks Association, 1991.

Jay, Tom and Brad Matsen. *Reaching Home: Pacific Salmon, Pacific People*. Bothell, WA: Alaska Northwest Books, 1994.

Morley, James. *Muir Woods: The Ancient Redwood Forest Near San Francisco*. San Francisco: Smith-Morley, 1991.

Steelquist, Robert. *Field Guide to the Pacific Salmon*. Seattle, WA: Sasquatch Books, 1992.

SCIENTIFIC

Groot, C. and L. Margolis. *Pacific Salmon Life Histories*. Vancouver, Canada: University of British Columbia Press, 1991.

Groot, C., L. Margolis, and W. C. Clarke, ed. *Physiological Ecology of Pacific Salmon*. Vancouver, Canada: University of British Columbia Press, 1995.

Hasler, A. D. and A. T. Scholz. *Olfactory Imprinting and Homing in Salmon: Zoophysiology*. New York: Springer-Verlag Press, 1983.

Heath, Alan. *Water Pollution and Fish*. Boca Raton, FL: CRC Press, 1995.

Rogers, David. "Pattern and Process in Large-Scale Animal Movement." In *The Ecology of Animal Movement*. Oxford: Clarendon Press, 1984.

Usinger, R. L. *Aquatic Insects of California, with Keys to North American Genera and California Species*. Berkeley: University of California Press, 1956.

TECHNICAL

California Department of Fish and Game. "California Salmonid stream habitat restoration manual," 1994. Copy located at National Park Service Resource Management Office, Fort Cronkhite.

"Endangered and threatened species: threatened status for central California coast coho salmon, Evolutionary Significant Unit (ESU), October 31, 1996. Federal Register 61(212) 56138-56149. Copy located at National Park Service Resource Management Office, Fort Cronkhite.

Khosla, Maya. "Redwood Creek Management Plan Draft." Muir Woods National Monument, Sausalito, CA, 1995.

Acknowledgments

A curious young visitor to Redwood Creek once asked, "Do the salmon get smaller again when they come up in here?" I owe him many thanks for that thought-provoking moment, which came as I wrestled with words to explain what returning salmon do. And I would like to thank Darren Fong, National Park Service aquatic biologist, who formulated the entire survey/assessment scheme according to important factors in aquatic life, including adult salmonid spawning and rearing, and trained us in habitat survey methods. Thanks also to Amy Lambert, who is always encouraging and energetic about questioning the creek measurements in new ways and who took part in a number of surveys. I appreciate Muir Woods ranger Mia Monroe for involving her interns in the surveys in such a big way; she has been in touch with this beautiful stretch of water for more years than most of us.

I thank Darren and Tina for doing much of the data recording downstream of the Muir Woods section of Redwood Creek; and Dan, Brian, Phil, Mark, and Mahalia for helping me with data collection at various points through Muir Woods. Sharon Farrell provided useful suggestions about the arrangement of this material, and Amy Lambert and David Hill made efforts to temper the manuscript's first flow with their comments, which were very encouraging!

*Your purchase contributes to the
conservation, improvement, and public enjoyment
of Golden Gate National Recreation Area.
Thank you for your support.*

— GOLDEN GATE NATIONAL PARKS ASSOCIATION